Mind Game

Mind Game

A QUANTUM PERFORMANCE LEAP FOR COMPETITIVE PICKLEBALL AND TENNIS

Neil P. Schulenburg

ISBN-13: 9780692756393
ISBN-10: 0692756396

Foreword

I f you are new to pickleball or tennis and need information about the rules of the game, effective court strategy, or the best grip to use on your racquet or paddle, this is probably not the book for you. If you have these things fairly settled and are interested in moving to the next level, this book may be just the thing to help you do so. Mastering the concepts that are presented here can make that next step for your game more like a quantum leap. I hope that you will give this a sincere try and become the best player that you can be.

What is contained in this work is centered on the mental aspects of these two court games. The mental activity is similar in both games, so the examples used to explain basic ideas might be situations from either sport.

If you are not sure that you are ready for a quantum-leap improvement in your game, read a little further.

What Kind of Player Are You?

f it is set point or championship point, and you are serving to win, do you

a.   serve your best ace of the match?
b.   serve up a fault? If you're going to fault, this is where it will happen. At best, it will be a half-speed push that will likely lead to a lost opportunity.

If it is a long rally, the exchange of shots is evenly matched and the test is "who will blink first," are you

a.   the one who can "will" the opponent into submission? You don't rely on your big weapons. You rely on your steady determination.
b.   the one who usually becomes anxious and tries to take the offensive shot even when the opportunity isn't there? You just have to

break out of the unresolved moment, even if you end up losing the point.

Are you fairly happy with the way you play when you're "on"?

a. When I'm "feeling it" and having an "on day," I feel like I can compete with anyone. When I'm not "on" and "feeling it," I know what to do to get there.
b. Sometimes I just can't find it. I try hard to focus and get my game back, but I get into these streaks where everything is either going long or going into the net. I usually end up quitting for the day.

Are you happy with your doubles performance?

a. We play as if we are better than a well-oiled machine. We play in what feels like perfect synchronization. Our teamwork allows us to maximize our court coverage at all times.
b. My partner and I are at the top of our games as individuals, but can't seem to put it all together as a team during competition. Players that we both beat in singles beat us in doubles.

If you answered "b" to any to the questions above, it is likely that this book can make a significant difference in your game. All those hours spent in training for fitness and practice on the court perfecting shot mechanics can be superseded by one often-overlooked factor, the mental game.

During the 1980s and 1990s Chris Everett would amaze tennis fans around the world with her mental game. If the match got tough, she got tougher. Along came Martina Navratilova with her athleticism and arsenal of shots. Chris would still dominate. That is, until Martina developed the same iron will to win. Then Martina was unstoppable.

Where does this ability come from? At the time, it seemed that Chris was born with it. Martina showed the tennis world that it can be developed as with other tennis skills.

It is my hope that the ideas presented here will awaken what is perhaps the most significant aspect of your game, the mind game.

Endorsements

The serve was the weakest part of my game. I would love to play, but when it came time for me to serve I felt tremendous pressure. I hit way too many serves out. After using the techniques outlined in this book, the serve became one of the strongest parts of my game. A spectator recently told me, "When you're serving, you're so consistent you look like a machine out there." ...That's no machine, that's the real me!
—Pickleball and Tennis player, St. Simons Island, GA

When I read this book I found that I couldn't put it down. I read it all in one day. I could really relate to this...I found things that I hadn't considered before.
—Frank Solana, Tennis Professional,
St. Simons Island, GA

Acknowledgements

T hanks go to a number of very helpful people who have been instrumental in the development of this work. First, I am grateful for the understanding that my wife Kathryn has shown as I have invested time in the sports of pickleball and tennis. She has spent a great deal of her energy in the editing process for this book as well. I would also like to thank other good friends that have contributed their skills as this work was developed. Both Allison Cox and Lorraine Coiro were generous with their time and support. Cathy Foley was a steady source of positive energy. Thanks to Frank Solana for providing his perspective from the tennis players view point. My long-time friend Richard Newquist provided the catalyst of enthusiastic encouragement which is so important for a creative project.

The pickleball and tennis players from Saint Simons Island, Georgia, and the members of the Golden Isles Pickleball Society have always been helpful and willing to share their knowledge of the game. Thanks to all.

Contents

Foreword · v

What Kind of Player Are You? · vii

Endorsements · xi

Acknowledgements · xiii

Introduction · xvii

Chapter 1   Where Are You "Headed"? · 1

Chapter 2   The Zone—Not the Twilight Zone · · · · · · · · · · · · · · · · · · 7

Chapter 3   Avoidance Can Be a Good Thing · · · · · · · · · · · · · · · · · · · 19

Chapter 4   Now We're Clicking! · 29

Chapter 5   Gamesmanship—The Dark Side of the Force · · · · · · · · · · · · 39

Chapter 6   How to Set the Stage ································43

Chapter 7   External Factors that Influence the Zone—Tomatoes
and Kudos···53

Chapter 8   What Is It Like to Be in the "Zone" or Experience That
"Flow"?···57

Appendix I Practice Drills···61

Real Life Examples ································71

Note to the Reader ································73

Further Reading ································75

Notes - How and Why ································77

About the Author ································83

Introduction

Pickleball and tennis are sports for all ages and skill levels. Involvement usually begins as a leisure activity. It's just fun to get out on the court and have a few laughs with friends. For most players, it soon begins to dawn on them that these are real sports. They are great for exercise, and court games take real skill and some thoughtful strategy. After a while, new players begin to develop a desire to improve their skill level, so they can show their friends that they can play a competitive game.

For some of us, the desire continues to grow. We might begin to have an interest in participating in some local tournaments. Some may go all the way and become competitive nationwide. Regardless of the level of competitive interest, the idea of playing our best and winning becomes a key part of our love for the sport.

This book is not about the mechanical skills that are required. It's not about the strategy either. Our focus will be about what goes on in our brain when we play a winning game and what goes on when we don't.

It has been said that aptitude in recreational sports like pickleball and tennis is 90 percent about what takes place between our ears. If that's the case, maybe we should spend a little more time thinking about what we're doing in that area.

The focus of this book will be about that 90 percent factor which is mental or emotional. Is there really a right and wrong way to play a recreational sport from a mental standpoint? It's my belief that the mental part of the game does indeed play a much larger part in our performance than we acknowledge.

Some general principles of neurological function will be discussed as they relate to sports performance. We will also address some specific "dos and don'ts" in the games of pickleball and tennis. The objective is to provide some real suggestions that can maximize your performance.

The characters identified in this book are composite personalities and are comprised of a number of characteristics from several real-life individuals. No persons named are actual individuals. The characters included here are fictitious and are used in this book for illustration purposes only.

CHAPTER 1

Where Are You "Headed"?

While writing this book, I am making an effort to keep up my exercise and hone my skills as best I can in my chosen game and at my level of play. About eighteen months ago, I made a transition from tennis to pickleball. I had to leave tennis due to some health restrictions and I was brokenhearted over it. I have had a love for tennis my entire adult life. When I was introduced to pickleball, I had a pretty standard reaction. I thought that it couldn't be a serious sport with a name like that. What followed for me was a rapid entry into a new world of fulfillment on the playing court. Today I am "all in" in the world of pickleball. I still love tennis and continue to be a fan. Even so, there is a special place in my heart for pickleball. I feel that it rescued me from the potential of losing court games from my life all together.

Recently, I had the opportunity to team with someone who competes in tournaments at a 4.5 level. According to the USAPA ratings (USA Pickleball Association), people at that level are very proficient players. This player is one notch away from 5.0, which would place him close to the very top of the ranking system. For the sake of confidentiality, we will refer to him as Bob.

Bob was a joy to play with. Watching Bob move on the court with such ease and flowing motion could easily hypnotize a casual observer of the game. But, as the game unfolded, some things began to happen that didn't seem to fit. He hit four shots out of bounds on his serve. There were also several missed shots from the ground and from volleying positions. We ended up losing the game and like a good sport, he apologized for his errors. The rest of us provided support with the usual, "It happens to all of us. It's just an off day."

The truth of the situation is that, rather than dismissing it, we would all like to know what made it an off day so that we can avoid it in the future. In this situation, it was a consistent pattern of what I call brain-state violations. The next chapter will address an optimum brain-state condition that some sports psychologists call the "Zone" or "Flow." For now, let's just consider the possibility that there may be an optimum state of mind for peak performance.

When Bob prepared to serve, you could see a grim expression on his face. It appeared as though he was focusing as hard as he could on the mechanics of his serve and trying hard not to lose the point by faulting. His intentions were good. He was trying his best to execute the shot, but the result was disastrous. His intense concentration was taking him to a mental state that was not conducive to athletic performance. He certainly had the required skills and experience to be successful. Looking at the situation as a third party observer, it seemed that an unseen force was holding him back.

In addition to this issue with personal performance, something else was going on that had to do with the performance of his doubles partnership. His competitive drive led him to some verbal coaching that also had disastrous results. On several occasions, a particularly difficult shot would present itself and with all the good intentions in the world, Bob would shout out "you're there" or "easy shot." Without realizing it, he was holding himself and his partner back with one brain-state violation after another.

With some new habits designed to guard the appropriate brain state, Bob could easily compete and win at the 5.0 level of play. If that's true, let's spend a little time discussing that optimum brain state.

CHAPTER 2

The Zone—Not the Twilight Zone

Many sports psychologists refer to the optimum brain state for athletic performance as being in the "Zone." Mihaly Csikszentmihalyi, a Hungarian psychologist, has been credited with originating this term. Some refer to it as "Flow." Flow or being in the Zone is experienced when a person is aware that they have arrived at a level of performance that they sense is ideal. The motions of the activity seem to flow naturally from one movement to the next. Time doesn't seem to matter. It's all about feeling very natural without any conscious effort involved. When athletes compete while they are in the Zone, they describe it as an experience when conscious thought was not taking place. To them, it was all about the feeling of being completely saturated in the present moment. Their bodies seemed to move in perfect synchronization with the feeling as if it was a dream. They were not allowing any form of conscious thought to interfere with the feeling of being in that zone of performance.

My first experience with playing in the zone came quite by accident. It was twenty years ago and my game at that time was tennis. I was living in Atlanta, which had the reputation of having more tennis players and tennis courts per square mile than any American city. It seemed that our

whole life revolved around tennis and social events that were with our teammates. We dedicated a lot of time to practice through the week and then to serious competition in league play on the weekends.

With that as the backdrop, I'll attempt to explain how this encounter with the zone took place. There was an evening practice, one fine Atlanta night, when the zone manifested itself in striking clarity. My friend John and I were the first two members of the team to show up for practice. He was one of our top players. He always played in the number one position. We began to hit the ball back and forth just to get warmed up. Soon it was noticeable that we were both pushing the envelope, hitting deep shots from corner to corner. Without conscious thought, I became aware that we were both slamming the ball with terrific force on every shot. Both of us moved with perfect timing to hit the ball back with what seemed to be effortless rhythmic movement. I didn't want the practice to end. I'm sure that John felt the same way. After a time (I have no idea how much time), another one of our best players showed up. As he moved to the court next to us, he shouted out with a sarcastic kind of humor, "Why don't you guys hit the ball a little harder"? With that comment I knew that I had stumbled on something special, a mind state that is worthy of relentless pursuit.

If we have any hope of achieving that state of mind we need to know more about what it is, how to get there and how to stay there. If it is a feeling, then we need a way to activate the feeling mechanisms in our brain.

Before we go too much further with the concept of an optimum brain state, let's apply some common sense. To illustrate, let's imagine that you were going to attempt to learn a new motor skill. In the process, there are certain steps that you would take. Let's use the example of learning to ride on a unicycle. Your intention might be to develop this skill to a level of proficiency that would allow you to ride in the upcoming July Fourth parade. It is likely that you would talk to a number of people who have mastered this activity. You would read as much as you could about the correct way to ride on this very different and challenging device. It is not likely that you would take off as soon as you had completed reading the instructions. You would probably learn about the mechanics of riding a unicycle the way that you would read the instructions before you assemble a model airplane, but reading the instructions would not be enough. You would then venture slowly into basic riding skills by doing simple and safe motions. There would be repetition as you "groove" the new skills. It would be important to learn what the proper mechanics of riding actually feel like. The repetition would record in your mind what that effective mechanical skill feels like experientially. We do this so that we can repeat the effective movements and discard the ineffective. Some call this building muscle memory. I view muscle memory to be a recording of what the movement feels like.

If it is true that we need to include that experiential aspect of learning in our training plan as we begin a new sport, then why do so many of us revert back to following the detailed instructions (shot mechanics, specific tactics, etc.)? We say to ourselves things like, "Keep your head down," "turn your shoulders," "watch the ball." It's as if we are forcing a behavior through our intellect (logical brain activity) as opposed to allowing our mind and body to do what comes naturally (feeling the activity as it is recorded in our memory).

Much has been written in the sports psychology literature on the topic of the Zone. Most of the information that I have seen is about relaxation and how to promote a state of mindfulness by shutting out distractions. My viewpoint is a little different in that, it comes from a neurological perspective that is based on the general functions of the left and right side of our brain.

Left-Brain Hemisphere		Right-Brain Hemisphere
Sequential processing		Visuospatial processing
Verbal/graphical		Almost mute
Logical		Emotional/feelings

It is my theory that, to perform at our best, we need to become more right brained than left. In general terms, the left hemisphere of our brain is sequential in the way that it processes things. It is very verbal and logical. Our right hemisphere is more visuospatial in the way it processes information, emotional, and almost totally mute. If we are intending to arrive at a brain state that is associated with a feeling, a sense of timelessness with an absence of verbalization, then it seems appropriate to stay in the right brain as much as possible.

If this theory (based on the functions of the right and left hemispheres) is correct, it would be advantageous to an athlete to be able to turn it on and off at will. Have you ever had trouble remembering the score when you are serving? When this has happened to me in the past, I would usually just tell myself that I was tired and that I would have to concentrate harder. Sometimes I've found myself unable to verbalize a simple sentence after a long rally. Again, I have typically told myself that I was just getting older and having what is referred to as a senior moment. What if what is really happening in these times is a result of becoming right-brain dominant? We may have found our way into a brain state conducive to performance during competition and then were unable to switch back to the logical and verbal aspects of brain function quickly enough to respond in time.

Pickleball and tennis require the server to announce the score before the serve is delivered. This verbal task takes us in the opposite direction of where we need to go in order to do our best with the serve. Announcing the score is logical and verbal by nature and is primarily a left-brain function. In order to begin the point, we need to be able to play back recordings of the feelings associated with effective movement during a serve. Those feelings would be visuospatial and right-brain oriented. We need the ability to move from the verbal left to the feeling right as an intentional shift and then back again as an act of our will.

In the last chapter, we could see the wheels falling off Bob's game for some reason that was unknown at the time. Let's look at what happened from the perspective of being in or out of the Zone.

When Bob stood at the line to serve, he was doing his best to concentrate. He was reviewing in his mind all the proper mechanics of his serve. He was probably telling himself to put the ball in play without making an error. Just before he started his motion, he was focusing his attention on his serve as much as possible.

What could possibly be wrong with that? We are all taught to do things like that, as we learn how to play a sport. What many of us miss is that there is a transition that is required when moving from the practice court to the playing court for competition. There is one brain state for learning and another for effective play.

The problem that Bob was running into was that all of his shot preparation was left-brained activity. With all of that taking place, he was shutting himself out of the Zone of optimum performance. With his analytical brain running at top speed, there was little opportunity to enter that dreamlike state.

A better way to handle this frustrating situation is to journey through a series of tasks that lead us to the appropriate brain state. It's OK to review your mechanics when you realize that there is a problem, but don't get stuck there. The review is a left-brained activity, so make that something that you do early in your preparation and then leave it. Go as quickly as possible to your right brain. This is the most important skill that an athlete can develop to enhance their performance regarding the metal aspect of the game. With well-developed skills in this area players can make a significant step up in performance overall. What we are developing is the ability to make an intentional shift from using our brain to process what the shot is logically (a set of specific movements represented by verbal descriptions and graphic representations) to what the shot is like when it is experienced (simply a progression of feelings).

A shot is hit and missed. Next, there is a flood of counterproductive thoughts that are activated. Was it a good shot selection? (left brained, logical appraisal of value). Were my mechanics sound? (left brained, a review of graphics or verbal representations) Did I disappoint my partner? (left brained with a bleed over to the wrong right-brain activity) We could lose the tournament on this shot (left brained, thinking of the future, not in the here and now) I've been hitting that shot poorly all morning (left brained, stuck in the past). Maybe I'm not as good as I think I am. ...

Left-Brain Hemisphere		Right-Brain Hemisphere
Sequential processing	I	*Visuospatial processing*
Could lose (future)		Not engaged here and now
Same mistake (past)		Not processing surroundings
Verbal/graphical	I	*Almost mute*
Sound mechanics?		Chatter makes it difficult to shift.
Logical	I	*Emotional/feelings*
Good shot selection?		Disappoint my partner?
		(negative)
		Could lose (negative)

Let's think about ways to recover from a missed shot. Most of the initial thoughts listed above are automatic. Like it or not, these thoughts will compete for center stage in our mind. It's up to us to recognize that we are being pulled in the wrong direction and then take conscious steps to change things.

Let's make some adjustments to how your mind works.

The Fix

First, take proactive measures to reduce stress. Without a cool head, it is difficult to move from one brain state to another. There are a number of ways to accomplish this. It is beyond the scope of this book to cover stress reduction comprehensively. Let's just assume that you have some basic skills in this area already. Now is the time to use what is in your arsenal. Sometimes reminding yourself to breathe deeply and methodically will be enough. Alternate tapping on both sides of your body can be an effective way to de-stress. There is a professional tennis player from Canada, Vasek Pospisil, who does this regularly. He will sit on the bench on change overs with a towel over his head as he alternately taps his right thigh and then his left. When he does this, he is utilizing a skill that is taught by psychothera-pists who employ the mode of therapy called EMDR or Eye Movement Desensitization and Reprocessing. It allows him to reset his emotions and come back to compete at his highest level of performance.

Next, get into your right brain. To do this, you have to leave all the above-mentioned thoughts behind. A good approach is to play effective and truthful statements in your mind. You can remind yourself that there is a proper place for left-brained thinking. That place is in the first part of your preparation for the next shot. Since it has been addressed and is in its proper place, then you can move on. Playing the wrong message over and over only predestines the next effort to failure. To activate the right brain, you can visualize your shot happening. Don't stay there, because the intentional part of that activity requires left-brain effort. Once you have visualized the shot, it's time to *immerse yourself in the feeling*.

On the serve, don't take the shot until you're feeling it. We can learn something more from professional tennis in this area. Rafa Nadal will go down in history as one of the best tennis players of all time. He takes a painfully long time in his preparation before he serves. He is going through a ritual or a predetermined sequence of actions. The sequence is always the same, whether it is the first point of the match or the last. This is recommended by many coaches, but why is this so important? As Rafa moves through his routine, he is able to let go of the thoughts involved in the motions. Since it is the same every time he serves, he is freed from that sequential thought process and can allow his competitive best to come to the forefront by simply feeling the shot.

In the middle of a rally (a back and forth exchange of shots), stay with what the rhythm of play *feels* like. This situation is different from the serve in that you are not initiating the shot. You are reacting. You don't have the time for rituals because the action is ongoing. This is where you play the role of gatekeeper. When thoughts creep in that you know do not belong, do everything in your power to dispense with the thought and move back to feeling the flow again. You might be saying to yourself that this recommendation is easier said than done. I agree completely. That is why it's important to drill this mental exercise in much the same way that you drill the mechanics of one of your strokes. When the extraneous thought creeps in, take it captive by not allowing it to play.

Take it captive by challenging it. Key words that identify the problem like, "future," "mechanics," or "worries" can identify the issue. Then you can dispense with it by replacing it with something useful that will allow you to reenter the Zone. For example, the word "ball" spoken internally will bring you back to the here and now. It will give your left brain something relatively simple to do while you are turning the emphasis of brain activity over to your feeling-oriented right side. Search your memories for what that next shot feels like when you have executed it flawlessly in the past. Play the thought purposefully as if it was a favorite tune. Then move along with the memory as if you are duplicating it perfectly as you follow the flow of feelings.

Another trick I have seen employed in professional tennis is a slap on the left thigh. Maria Sharapova does this often. When she does this, it is more than just a way to maintain her level of arousal. Since we are cross wired in our nervous system, she is activating her right brain; bringing it online so that she can be immersed in the feeling of her shots. She has a number of good habits that allow her to maximize her performance. Another noticeable habit of hers is taking the time to reset her mind state by facing the rear of the court before beginning the next point. This gives her the opportunity to shift gears mentally.

I have employed that technique at the amateur level and have gotten some good laughs from my opponents. On one occasion, while I was facing the fence instead of the other players, they shouted to me, "hey…we're over here"! The trick is to let them laugh all they want. Believe in what you are doing enough to put it into practice regardless of what others think. In the end, you will be going home with the medals and they will be wondering how you did it.

CHAPTER 3

Avoidance Can Be a Good Thing

I n this chapter, we'll cover some common mistakes to avoid. The purpose is to become more aware of the mental aspect of the game, the part of the game that so often gets lost in the shuffle of competition. It's difficult to address mistakes without offending players who may see their own behavior in these descriptions. As you read on, keep in mind that the overall objective is for all of us to become better players, learners, and coaches. None of us has arrived at a state of perfection. If that ever happens, then it will no longer be a game and we'll all lose interest.

Go...go! (and away goes the point)

What would we do without the advanced players who help us get to be better competitors? We need their help to move up to the next level of play. Sometimes these important people, in their enthusiasm and with their advanced court sense, interfere with the mental aspect of the game. To be fair, this is not their intention.

Here is the situation on the pickleball court. (Tennis players skip this paragraph)

Finally, you have a chance to play a game with the top player in the club. He has all the shots and could easily play at the top levels in tournament play. You are serving. The shot goes in and is returned to you. You let it bounce as required by the rules and hit an intermediate level shot back to the other side. You are pleased that you kept the ball in play and advance toward the non-volley zone line on your side of the court. The opponent is able to place the ball short and is advancing more quickly to their non-volley zone line. Acutely aware of the situation, your partner shouts out "Go...Go"! There are many other words that can be used in this verbal exhortation such as "Yours!" or "Up!" All of them have the same effect.

Here's a similar situation on the tennis court. (Pickleball Players skip to the next paragraph - The Bitter End)

After many hours spent on the practice court, you finally have a chance to play with one of the best players in your club. You are serving and hitting the ball well. During a hotly contested point, you end up in a crosscourt exchange with your opponent from the baseline. You both are hitting sharp angled shots with a lot of power. The players at the net have not been able to cut off the exchange. The rally continues until you hit a shot that is shallow, setting up the opponent with several options. He elects to throw in a drop shot. You see the shot coming and feel that you have it covered. Your partner panics when he realizes that you are not yet in position at the net. In an attempt to preempt disaster your partner shouts out, "Come up...Come up"!

The Bitter End

You read the shot well, you get to the ball in plenty of time, but you miss hit the easy shot. It goes directly into the net.

What happened? The advanced player is technically correct. You should move forward as quickly as possible in that situation. He's only trying to help. In your case, you may have felt that you are naturally a step faster than most people at your age and skill level and that you had everything under control.

You hear a "hrrrumph ..." from your playing partner as he moves back to his position for the next play. We'll talk about that in detail later on, but for now, let's consider what happened in this situation and that 90 percent factor of the game that we have agreed is mental. What resulted from his well-intentioned interjection was a brain-state violation. When he shouted out, you were plucked cleanly and immediately out of the Zone. Feeling the shot with your right brain was suddenly replaced with left-brained activity. "Am I making a mistake"? "Is he right"? "Am I good enough to play with him"? "Maybe he won't want to play with me after this." "I should have moved sooner." Even the fact that you're forced to process a verbal command takes you back to the left brain. Operating out of the left side took you out of the desired state for *feeling the perfect volley.*

We have to be able to communicate if we want to be successful in team sports like doubles pickleball and tennis. There is a right time and a wrong time to allow your team to do this. If you are one of those advanced players who uses this technique, I hope that you are not offended by this viewpoint. I'm sure that your intention has been to help others to play better. Just let me suggest that this technique should be used sparingly. It is a good practice to agree with the person in need of coaching that this kind of help is going to be coming their way. If they have a bad habit of hanging back at the base line, get their permission to coach them during the rally. Keep in mind that they will be in a compromised situation mentally if you do this. Agree together that this is a good training aid while a new behavior is being reinforced. Remember to leave it on the practice court when you are in a serious competitive situation.

Just Get It In!

This kind of advice is common from players at all levels of the game. It is another well-intentioned suggestion that results in disaster much of the time. When this happens, we laugh it off and repeat the same error over and over.

Again, the coaching player is just trying to help. He wanted to take some pressure of you by inferring that you don't need a fantastic serve to win. You stand at the service line with that thought in mind and proceed to hit the ball directly into the net.

You're not surprised. Further, you are more than a little miffed, because that was exactly what you were trying to avoid. Then comes the confusion. Why does this happen to me? You are clearly in a different state of mind after the error. Could it be that I started from the wrong state? What was my thought just before the serve?

In tennis, there is an old adage that says "Never say 'don't double fault.'" If you do, you visualize the double fault, feel that double fault, and have successfully programmed yourself to execute the perfect double fault.

The same is true for pickleball. Telling your partner to "just get it in" sets off a cascade of left-brained activity that leads you down the primrose path to failure. You begin to think about what it means to "just get it in". You focus on how important it is to "just get it in". In the end you are paralyzed by how badly you want to "just get it in", and so on.

We will address the best possible behavior in partners' relationships later but a good thought for the partner is to pose the internal question;

"What does my partner need most at this time?" We will see that the most beneficial contribution from a partner is unconditional acceptance. This makes it possible for the player receiving help to reset their mental and emotional activity, clearing the way for *feeling* the winning shot.

Coaching During the Game

All communication should take place in a very controlled manner. The key is to determine what is appropriate. Match strategy is critical and should be well coordinated with a doubles team. There is a subtle difference between strategizing with your partner and coaching. During the flow of the game, if you take the time to cross the line into coaching you are dragging your partner back to the practice court when he or she is supposed to be fully present on the playing court.

A good rule of thumb is to avoid what might make your partner self-conscious. Place a priority on things that might build team confidence. Things that you agree upon in the area of court strategy have the potential to build confidence when you work on them together.

If you notice that your opponents have been slow coming forward you might make that observation and agree to push them back and then go with a drop shot. You may notice that one of the opponents is particularly adept on their forehand side and agree to hit to the other side of the court.

Things to avoid are any adjustments to stroke mechanics like bending your knees more on low volleys. That's good advice but could trap your partner in his or her left brain and make it impossible for him or her to play their best game.

Hrrrrumph!

Let's consider the impact of your own response to your partner's errors. If you do *anything* that is negative, you are dragging your partner out of the Zone and into all kinds of competing brain activity.

Your job is to maintain an environment that is conducive to success. It is obvious that negative behavior is going to be counterproductive to our state of mind. It is important to note that silence can be equally damaging. In order to stay in the Zone, your partner needs to know that you are there in a positive way. Next, we'll address how to do this without disturbing that mystical state of mind called the Zone.

Just Plain Mad!!!

Every so often, maybe with one in one hundred players, anger surfaces in the course of competition. It's usually more like an eruption. There is some kind of trigger. It could be a mistake made by the player themselves, a questionable call by their opponents or an error committed by that person's partner. There may be loud verbal venting of the anger. Worse than that, the anger response may be directed at someone on the court. Sometimes rackets or paddles are thrown with great force into the net or smashed to the ground.

In all of these situations the result is the same. The dramatic display of emotion dominates the moment and all concerned have to struggle to find a way back to the Zone. Most of the time the other players involved stand back and let the storm pass. The other players begin to resent the angry player for ruining their outing, with what is supposed to be a "fun sport".

So then, if this is something that happens in a small number of players, why bring it up in a discussion of maximizing our performance? In short, if you play enough, you will encounter this type of player and when you do, you will have a decision to make. Do I let the bad behavior color my entire experience today or should I do something to change things?

My recommendation is to take action. Most of us see the display of negative emotions and think that the person is just acting like an adolescent and should clean up their attitude and their behavior. If they are repeat offenders some decide to just avoid playing with that person. I've seen this play out in sudden displays of disgust where the offended person just walks off the court leaving everyone in the lurch.

In clinical settings this problem comes up often in marriage relationships. People come in for counseling knowing that their anger is destroying their home life but have little control over their behavior. It is more than adolescent misconduct. In these situations, anger management counseling is strongly recommended. A professional counselor may also recommend EMDR (Eye Movement Desensitization and Reprocessing). EMDR can resolve early life experiences that remain as hidden heart wounds. An example of that would be someone who endured taunting and emotional abuse from an authority figure like a parent, coach or sibling. These traumatic experiences become emotional landmines. When someone in the present-day experience causes a familiar echo from the angry person's abusive past, pain and eventually anger are the result. The anger is spewed outward toward anyone and anything in the way.

The first thing to do is to recognize the situation and take action to maintain your brain state. Your job is to remain present in the here and now, remain separated from the unfolding drama, stay relaxed, and continue to feel the rhythm of the moment in the match. There are lots of ways to do that. Now is the time to use the tools that work best for you.

It's also a good idea to set some reasonable goals for your group regarding how to deal with the situation. I don't believe that the answer is to ignore the problem. I've seen problem situations like this persist for years in some groups. Everyone knows that when John comes to play the climate is delicate and likely to turn negative. When the problem is ignored it is likely to remain unchanged.

I don't believe that threats of excommunication are helpful either. When people struggle with anger outbursts it is an outward sign of a behavior disorder that can be resolved through appropriate forms of psychotherapy. The trick is how to explain this to the person with the problem. Most of us don't want to take a chance that we will become the next target of their anger. It may be best to have one of the players who the affected person respects the most bring the suggestion to him or her. It may be appropriate for several in the group to have a private and positive meeting resembling an intervention in the treatment of addictions. One way or the other the affected person needs help. With the right kind of help these negative echoes from the past that have continued to haunt him or her can be naturally and effectively resolved. It is up to you. Eliminate the anger problem and gain a "new" playing partner or ignore the problem and accept that there will be interruptions during play and brain state violations requiring all your best skills to maintain your place in the Zone.

CHAPTER 4
Now We're Clicking!

What does appropriate court behavior look like? Managing behavior can have a dramatic effect on whether or not we are playing in the Zone. First of all, putting the practice time in will build a special level of familiarity with your partner's game. Have you ever watched how beautifully coordinated a professional basketball team can play? On a fast break, the team with the ball moves down the court in a precise formation. The player with the ball is in the lead but he knows that several defensive players are very close behind him. With split second timing, the ball is flicked behind his back and into the hands of his teammate who has a clear path to the goal. The result is an easy slam dunk. It's beautiful to watch. The player who passed the ball off just knew without looking where his teammate would be. That kind of "just knowing" comes with many hours of practice time.

This knowledge of where your partner will be is important in tennis and pickleball when you think about court coverage. Some teams play as if they are two independent players with their own personal areas of responsibility. This is my side and that is yours. There is little contact and scant communication. Other teams seem to flow together as a unit. Some have described their movement to be as if they had a rope tied to their waists between them and they move perfectly in tandem. Then, at just the right time there is a change. One of the partners sees an opportunity for a poach, taking the ball on their partner's side of the court, and hitting the court player's version of a slam dunk. It's beautiful to watch, but the other player can't afford to just take it all in. As the poaching player moves across to the other side to take the winning shot, the other player moves in unison to cover the vacated court space by "switching," or crossing behind the poacher.

Those maneuvers take practice, but are well worth the effort. If, by some miracle, the "slam dunk" comes back, it will be a weak shot. It is likely that the ball will land in a place on the court that the opponent thought was a good shot selection, but found out the hard way that your team plays at a different level.

So how do we make sure that we look like that team that flows together in just the right place and at just the right time? Let's take a look at a good model from tennis. Doubles tennis at the professional level can be somewhat confusing to someone who doesn't know what is going on. There is so much contact with partners slapping hands at the end of each point. Then there is that endless chatter between partners. They have been playing for hours. They practically live together. What more could they possibly have to say to each other? Professionals have a deep appreciation for the importance of maintaining the connection with their partner. Their livelihood depends on this connection, so they do everything in their power to cultivate it. They know that if this connection starts to falter their performance will follow closely after.

Let's look at this behavior through the lens of effective brain-state management to see if we can improve our own performance. We'll start with what happens at the end of a point and work our way from there to the beginning of the next. What we will see at the end of a point is the two partners making eye contact with each other, moving toward each other and making contact with a hand slap. This solidifies their positive relationship. With their body language they are saying, "I'm with you no matter what." With regards to brain state, this is like buying some insurance that neither partner will fall into a left-brained process. If they are concerned about the last shot or even overly impressed with themselves, they are not poised for optimum performance.

Next, we see the partners walking back to the line together and having a little chat. You might be thinking that this seems to be a very left-brained activity. If so, you would be correct. Earlier, we said that there would be an appropriate time and place for communication. This is it. The last point is over. Now is the time for the partners to discuss game strategy. Remember that this is not the time for a lesson. They need a good strategy based on what they are seeing across the net. If one partner is serving, it is the other partner's job, after strategy is agreed upon, to reset his partner mentally.

A good habit is to have the server facing the rear of the court for the sake of clarity of purpose. A short word of encouragement like, "we're doing great." Then allow him or her to get mentally ready. The non-serving partner may remind the server of the sequence; visualize it, *feel it*, and then go with it. After the reminder, he should get out of the way.

Are We Really a Team?

Teaming is about more than being able to win a few games together. If you have some athletic ability, chances are that you can play with most other people at your level with a reasonable level of success. What if you want the optimum level of success for your skill level? It should be apparent by now that in order to approach peak performance, that 90 percent factor that we classified as mental/emotional must be a priority. All that we do has to make a positive contribution to getting to and staying in the Zone.

As mentioned earlier, there are several habits that are clearly a negative and some things that can be helpful. It is my opinion that there is something foundational that can keep us on the positive side. That foundation is the partner relationship. When this factor is in place and functioning properly, we feel a certain level of assurance that no matter what happens, our partner will be there for us. In mental health circles, this is sometimes referred to as unconditional positive regard. Some people use the term grace. However you refer to it, if we know that our teammate will extend that grace to us no matter what happens, it will set us free. That freedom enables us to do all the things that we need to do as individuals to stay in the Zone.

A good team can weather the storms that come. Whether you are referring to a marriage or a sports team, the bottom line regarding performance is dependent upon the strength of the relationship. When a problem presents itself, can you trust that your partner will stay positive and support you? Can you afford to make a mistake? Whether it is about a bad shot or a depressed and irritable mood, do you have the confidence that your partner will stick it out and work through it with you? If you don't, my advice is to work toward strengthening your relationship. If your partner has no interest in doing the hard work that is involved in forming a strong working relationship, then I would move on with someone who is willing.

As outlined earlier, there are enough pitfalls in the game that pull us out of the Zone without adding concerns about partner relationship drama. The opponent is on the other side of the net. We don't need another one on our side.

What follows is a short list of "how to"s" regarding relationship.

Be a Giver

Send a message to your partner, through your actions and your words, that says your priority is to sacrifice yourself for the betterment of your partner. We sacrifice of ourselves when we talk about what our partner wants to address and remain a good listener. Our every thought is about helping him or her. On every turn of events, forgiveness is extended and eventually becomes assumed. Your attitude should be that it doesn't matter that every ball your partner hits goes into the net. This isn't the time or place to correct faulty technique. This is the time to assure him or her that you have confidence in his or her skills and you are going to supply unwavering support.

Communicate (at the Appropriate Time)

To feel comfortable in any relationship, it is critical to be able to work our way through challenges. People make mistakes in the area of communication in two main ways. First, some people get aggressive. They make sharp sarcastic comments or vent their anger with a shout. This is clearly detrimental to the Zone of concentration. It whittles away the relationship as well. Relationships are comprised of trust. Each time that someone gets aggressive with us, we tend to trust him or her a little bit less. After all, they may do it again tomorrow. A second and equally damaging error is to be avoidant. This is where the offended party says nothing about their concern hoping that it will just go away. They might also decide that their personal needs are not important enough to address the issue. Either way, from that point forward, the avoidant person will be trying to play with a left brain that is focused on the past problem and a right brain that is flooded with negative emotions. He may feel hurt, angry, confused, or simply alone. All these things will take him or her to the wrong brain state.

Practice Together

When you practice, make it known to your partner that you are there to do the drills that he or she wants to work on. Your game is important too, but remember to do everything you can to send the message that you are committed to this relationship.

Avoid Infidelity

This may sound silly to you at first glance, but relationships can be fragile. Suppose that you and your regular partner make an agreement to stay together as a team for the entire season. In order to maximize the effectiveness of your play together, you make a verbal agreement to stay together. Shortly thereafter, a very special person becomes available to play with you in a tournament. He or she may be in town for a limited time and playing with them might be a great chance to finish in the medals. Just be mindful of the potential damage that can be done if you leave your regular partner high and dry even if it's just for one very special tournament. What you are seeing as the chance of your competitive lifetime may be far more damaging in the long run. Now your regular partner has a number of challenges. Self-doubt, anger, hurt, and more become major obstacles to success.

CHAPTER 5

Gamesmanship—The Dark Side of the Force

I f you are a sports fan, you are probably very familiar with the antics of tennis players like John McEnroe and Novak Djokovic. McEnroe was notorious for going into tirades, shouting at the umpire, and interrupting play. It was especially uncharacteristic for a game that was originally intended to be about sportsmanship. Early in his career, Djokovic would come down with mysterious illnesses at just the right time to interrupt the momentum of the game. It seems to some that these players are just acting in an immature manner. Both of these athletes are accomplished at the top of their sport. They have turned the tide in their favor on many occasions with their "playacting." The results have been major shifts in momentum in their favor. Perhaps, we all should learn more about how this happens so that we can insulate ourselves from these "back door" tactics.

Both of these men have a high level of awareness regarding the importance of the mental part of the game. Without attacking their opponent directly, they can yank them out of the Zone of peak performance with one of these tricks. If they can cause their opponent to become irritated, begin to imagine how nice it would be to beat a top player or win the match and thereby the tournament, they can shift the balance of competitive advantage to their side of the net. Their "antics" have actually drawn their opponents into left-brained activities where their performance will wither and die.

There is another player in professional tennis history who used this kind of mind manipulation of the opponent. It was seen with stark clarity in the game of Ivan Lendl. Lendl was number one in the world tennis rankings and the most dominant player of the 1980s. He was known for his blistering hot ground strokes and his icy cold personality. After a while, it became apparent that there was more going on with his winning record than good court strategy and solid shot mechanics. Lendl would actually attempt to hit his opponent with the ball even during the warm-up stage of the match. As shocking as that might sound to some tennis fans, the truth of the matter is he knew that gaining a leg up on his opponent mentally often makes all the difference. He knew that he wasn't really going to do physical damage with that fuzzy little ball, but by using that sort of "dirty trick," he might be able to do some damage to their mental game.

Why is this important to club players? It is commonly held that, at the club level, we're in our chosen sport for fun-loving and honest competition. Falling back to these kinds of tactics would be disgraceful! Or would it? Is it really inconceivable that in an important tournament, we could run into this type of behavior? Do we do some of these ourselves without giving it a thought?

I have to admit that I fell into this kind of attitude when I played tennis in Atlanta.

To the players in that area of the country, tennis was all about winning. We practiced hard and competed even harder. My game was at the stage where I had a pretty good level of confidence with all my shots. My objective at that time was to learn how to hit the ball with as much pace as I could possibly generate and still keep it in play. I could hit the ball with force on both sides but was especially comfortable with my backhand. On several occasions, I was able to hit the net player squarely in the chest with that shot, eliciting strong complaints from the opponent. At that time, we just laughed it off and bantered back that there was always the lower ranked team in the neighborhood that they could move down to if this level of play was too much for them. There are quite a few comments that we could make about that kind of tactic. Let's just say that performance was the priority even at the cost of relationship with neighbors and friends. Intimidation was an acceptable way to gain an edge on the competition.

For the most part, pickleball is a much more lighthearted game. I haven't seen much of that cold-blooded attitude in that sport. Even so, I have seen a strong desire to compete and win.

Whether the game is tennis or pickleball, when do we take a time out during a tournament? Do we exercise our right to a break when things are clicking in perfect rhythm and the points are adding up on our side? Never!

We take a break to regroup and try to shift the momentum of the match. This is not considered to be an underhanded tactic. Nevertheless, it can have a dramatic effect on performance and the outcome of a match. Take your time outs when you feel that your team has fallen out of the Zone of concentration. If your opponent takes a time out, do all that you can to preserve your state of mind. Remember to stay relaxed. *Don't focus on the past or advance to the future.* Have your strategy discussion with your partner but when you are done with that, visualize and *feel* your rhythm when things were going right. Don't begin playing until you are confident that you have taken the time to feel it.

CHAPTER 6
How to Set the Stage

Playing in the zone takes a conscious decision to do so. We have to activate the right brain with an intentional shift from the logical, sequential, and verbal left to the visuospatial, nonverbal, and more intuitive and emotional right. That may feel a bit like taking your hands off the handlebars of your bicycle. You may think that if you go with your feelings and neglect the thoughts about swing mechanics and potential outcomes then all will go to h... in a handbasket.

As we discussed earlier, game time is not the time for grooving shot mechanics or worrying about the potential points you will earn if you win. As Kenny Rogers says, "There's time enough for counting when the dealing's done." When you are in competition, you have to go with what you brought to the game that day. Doing anything that is left brained will drag you down and out of the Zone.

Assuming that we are going to engage the right brain as we play, let's consider what it takes to get ready. We have to clear the slate regarding what is currently playing in our mind. We want a very specific program to play so we have to make room for it. We can do that by quieting things down and doing some things to intentionally relax.

Herbs

Several herbal supplements can help with anxiety and stress. It has been known for some time that chamomile tea is relaxing and can help bring on a restful night's sleep. This might be a good tool to use the night before a match but we don't want to be sleepy on match day.

GABA is known to reduce anxiety. Unfortunately, it is difficult to get GABA to be absorbed in our bodies. Some supplement manufacturers market GABA in a form that is intended to be taken as drops administered under the tongue. If anxiety is a problem for you, then this might be worth a try.

Another supplement that is known to reduce anxiety and stress without causing drowsiness is L-Threonine. This amino acid is known to have a focused and relaxing effect. It will not put you to sleep when you need to be able to perform. I have used this in combination with GABA when I needed a little help to settle down from background stress and get ready for competition. The experience seems to be like turning the volume down on the "alarm system" in my mind. I am able to play in a relaxed state and perform at my best. Feeling the flow of the game and getting into the right brain state is easier with the background "noise" turned down.

PART (P.A.R.T.)

PART is an acronym used by cognitive psychotherapists to help their clients with anxiety. The letters stand for **p**repare, **a**cknowledge, **r**elax, and **t**ask. If you have performance anxiety before competition, this is a good cognitive tool to reduce the stress. Remind yourself that you have (P) prepared for this event. (A) Acknowledge that you feel some anxious feelings but that just gets you ready for action. (R) Relax intentionally by controlling your breathing or visualizing a relaxing place. Then (T) get on task. Place your equipment where it should be for the event. Stretch your muscles. Do your routine warm-up, and then just do it.

Activate Your Right Brain

Heart Math Inc. is an organization that provides products and methods to monitor and reduce stress. Their approach is to evaluate the level of stress as a function of heart-rate variability. The greater the variance in heart rate the greater the level of stress. Their equipment feeds that information back to the user in real time so they can refine their efforts to de-stress.

Their products are very effective. Their methods also seem to be in step with right- and left-hemisphere brain function. My interpretation of the approach to modifying heart-rate variability is as follows:

Close Your Eyes
Don't give your left brain anything to analyze.

Relax Your Muscles
Notice the difference between the *feeling* of being tense and the *feeling* of being relaxed (right brain).

Slow Your Breathing Down
Breathe in to the count of two heartbeats then out to the count of two heartbeats.
Slow breathing is associated with the *feeling* (right brain) of being relaxed.

Focus Your Attention on Your Physical Heart
This gives your left brain something simple to do so that it doesn't dominate with noisy chatter.

Feel a Few Moments of Deep Appreciation
Again, the emphasis here is on the word *feel*. You can start with a thought such as, I have a wonderful family or I'm so thankful that I was accepted at _____ University. Don't stay with the

thought! Just notice what it feels like to be appreciative. Enjoy that *feeling* (right brain).

This procedure can be used by itself or in conjunction with the monitoring equipment that is available through Heart Math. When you use the equipment, you have the ability to check your progress as you use the steps. If your stress level is not coming down, you can redirect your efforts.

Audio Visual Entrainment (AVE)

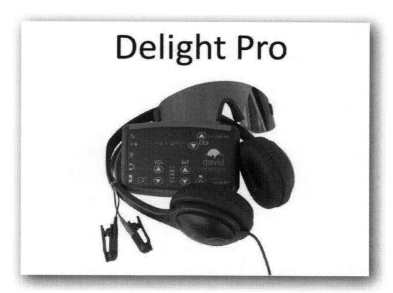

Meditation is a great way to bring about a relaxed state of mind. Unfortunately, meditation takes practice. After years of repetition, some can even slow their heart rate and influence their skin temperature just with the power of their mind. If you are good at this, it can put you way ahead of your competition. Unfortunately, most of us don't have years to wait for this skill to develop. A way to catch up if you haven't acquired this skill is to employ a method called Audio Visual Entrainment. This method employs a phenomenon first observed when radar technology was in the early stages of development. History reports that, in the early days of its use, radar operators would fall asleep on the job. This was not exactly conducive to a system that was intended to provide an early warning of an attack. It was a negative outcome at the time but it did stimulate some fruitful research. It was discovered that the brain would mirror certain frequencies when they are presented visually or as auditory signals. AVE technology introduces a desired frequency to encourage a desired brain state (meditation, sleep, concentration, etc.). If you want to induce a state of meditation before a big match, this can be an effective tool.

A number of professional athletes have used this technique with amazing results. If this sounds interesting to you, more information can be found at http://www.mindalive.com. This website provides supporting research information and testimonials from people who have been helped with this method. MindAlive offers equipment that has been shown to be effective both though clinical experience and through research. They offer several models including the Paradise and a new version the Delight Pro shown above.

Dave Siever, founder of MindAlive, tells the story of his first client in the area of sports performance.

The following are excerpts from their site:

The first athlete I helped use AVE to enhance sports performance was an amateur tennis player. He was experiencing pregame anxiety, which was costing him games because of mental mistakes and muscle fatigue. After using the DAVID Jr. for only one season, he was pleased to report to me that he had improved his overall standing from 150th place to 47th place.

Another story he shares is about a senior professional golfer.

Rocky Thompson worked relentlessly on the mechanics of his golf game, but it wasn't until he settled down some anxieties about his performance that he showed remarkable improvement. Two weeks after Rocky's introduction to the DAVID Paradise, he won at the Seniors Digital Classics in September of 1991. He attributed his win to the relaxation he benefited from using the DAVID Paradise. With his reduced stress level, his body was more relaxed and he was able to make better decisions. This also allowed him to deliver the shots he needed to win. Throughout his career, his anxiety cost him many games. But by becoming able to relax, he found that his body and mind were capable of playing the game at a higher level than he had previously thought possible.

It was reported that one of the senior golfers Rocky finished in front of in this event was the legendary Lee Trevino, one of the greatest American golfers of all time.

Eye Movement Desensitization and Reprocessing (EMDR)

Sometimes there is so much fear or anxiety involved that there is a temptation to give up. Some say to themselves in resignation, that they're just not meant for that kind of activity. This is common in competitive sports, music, acting, public speaking, and many other challenging situations. I don't believe in giving up. It is my nature to find solutions so that we can be the best that we can be in whatever we choose to do. It is my belief, confirmed by clinical experience and backed by research, that difficult experiences from our past can have a huge impact on our performance today. One of the pioneers of psychology, Alfred Adler, proposed an interesting concept regarding our memories. His idea was that we all carry forward those memories that we believe make us who we are. If he was right, then it is likely that the person who views himself or herself as "not a strong competitor" has something in their database of memories that confirms and drives that belief.

In the last thirty years, a new theory and mode of psychological intervention has emerged as being dramatically effective in the area of resolving difficult memories. That theory is AIP or Adaptive Information Processing. The intervention is called EMDR or Eye Movement Desensitization and Reprocessing. This relatively new form of treatment has been shown to be effective throughout the world in bringing healing to trauma victims from wars and natural disasters. In short, the method introduces various forms of stimulation that encourage the brain to deal with and put away troublesome memories. In their undigested form, these memories act like little land mines. As life comes along with its challenges, it finds one of those land mines, applies pressure, and causes an explosion of unwanted behavior. EMDR facilitates the natural processes that the brain goes through with normal memories, encouraging the brain to digest and clear away the difficult ones as well. The result is a brain that is no longer cluttered with undigested memories that can blow up in our face at the most inopportune time.

When the topic of trauma comes up, most people think of major disturbances that can be caused by extremely stressful situations. What escapes our awareness is the fact that trauma exists on a wide spectrum.

The originator of EMDR, Dr. Francine Shapiro explains this by using the terminology "big T" and "little t" trauma. Major disasters result in high-level or "big T" trauma. On the other hand, people will often exhibit behavioral repercussions from experiences in their lives that don't seem to be that significant. These lower-level types of experiences are considered to be little "t" trauma, but are still classified as trauma. For example, a therapist might point out to their client that an embarrassing experience that occurred many years in the past might have some significance with present day performance. The case might be from being embarrassed by a gym teacher in front of the whole class while in elementary school. The client might laugh a little and say that the memory was from long ago and that it never comes to mind anymore. Then during therapy, with a rush of confirming insight, the client comes to a significant level of understanding of himself or herself. Now it makes sense why they have been so intimidated by authorities at the gym and why they haven't had the determination to stick with and train for a new sport. This may be the reason why they have been so nervous when they are serving for the match or standing over that important putt. Clear away the land mines and clear away the potential interference from seemingly insignificant events from the past.

There is another situation that should be considered. Have you ever had the experience of being so anxious about a match that you couldn't seem to settle down? Have you ever been poised to deliver a serve and feel frozen in fear that you can't explain? Golfers often report falling into stretches of poor performance that seem to come out of nowhere. For these situations, a skilled EMDR psychotherapist can offer a potential solution. There may not be an obviously difficult memory from the past causing the difficulty, but the problem can still be addressed with EMDR by treating the troubling situation as an anticipated event. The problem situation might be the idea of having to serve out the last few points of a championship match. This anticipated experience can be defined with all of its characteristics like negative beliefs, negative emotions, and bodily response. That potential event can then be processed using the brain stimulation mentioned above and brought to resolution. After the therapy is completed, the client is able to face the situation in real life without the negative feelings that used to get in the way of peak performance.

That may sound pretty far-fetched to someone outside of the field of mental health. I can say with every conviction that I have seen and have had the privilege of facing these kinds of challenges with people with results that have appeared to be miraculous. People who have come to receive help with specific fears or simple self-esteem issues all report the same thing. The problem just disappeared. The fear is just gone. The frustration to the therapist is that many times the healing process feels too natural. The clients often report that the problem must have been less important than they thought. Perhaps it would have gone away on its own. At that point, the therapist is just happy that the client's goals have been realized. It really doesn't matter that the healing is perceived as just a natural event and is not always tied to the therapy they have received. The satisfaction is in seeing the client walk away free from what encumbered them in the past.

If this seems like an interesting approach and one that may be helpful, more information can be found at the EMDRIA (EMDR International Association) website http://www.emdria.com. This site contains useful information about EMDR along with a therapist search function that allows users to search for qualified therapists by geographic location.

CHAPTER 7

External Factors that Influence the Zone—Tomatoes and Kudos

Unfortunately, we don't live in a perfect world. Many things will compete for our attention and potentially "snatch defeat from the jaws of victory." What follows are a few of those unattractive moments that we all hope will go away someday. Tomatoes will be awarded to those making a negative impact and Kudos to those who are contributing positively.

Tomatoes go to the players on the sideline who are not conscious of other matches that are still under way. At times, noise from the socializing that takes place in the gallery bleeds over to the court where a match is in progress. It's fun to watch tennis and pickleball with all of the ups and downs. We sympathize with the player who misses and we celebrate with the ones who somehow pull off a miracle. Enjoy the matches, but don't create a problem for a match that is under way.

Kudos go to the gallery members who are aware of when to cheer and when to keep silent.

Rotten tomatoes go to the gallery member who feels compelled to make the line calls. Unless that person has been invited to take the responsibility of an umpire, calling the lines is the responsibility of the team on the side where the ball bounces.

Kudos go to the players on the sidelines who can allow the game to be played according to the rules.

More tomatoes can be awarded for this one. What is it like for you when you are about to serve at a critical time in a match and other players choose to walk directly behind your opponent to get to another court?

Kudos go to the player who stands and waits for the current rally to end and then asks for permission to cross behind the court.

A *Whole Bucket of Tomatoes* for this One! How about that unbelievable rally that goes back and forth far longer than anyone anticipates? Then suddenly someone hits a beautiful shot. In everyone's mind, the rally is over, but at the last second, your partner puts it in high gear and in a miraculous demonstration of foot speed, she is in the perfect place to recover the shot. The only problem is that someone (one of the opponents, someone from the sideline, or even your own partner) lets loose with a loud "Great shot!" or a groan before the rally is over. That sound completely destroys the fleet-of-foot player's experience of being in the Zone. She was there in the right position for the shot but the unaware enthusiast destroyed the moment.

We should all be having a good time, but let's not rob someone of their moment in the limelight. You should know that it is entirely acceptable to call a hindrance in this situation. Players hate to make that call because everyone involved is so taken by the excellence of play. There is usually a lot of laughter and congratulations offered. It's hard to play the spoiler role and say, "The shouting was a hindrance, we have to replay the point." You are liable to get some scowls from the person who hit the great shot, but don't sell yourself short. If the noise during the play interfered with your Flow or your ability to stay in the Zone, then call it. If more of us do so, then the people we play with will eventually honor our need to maintain our mind state and live a little closer to the rules of play.

Kudos go to the players who know when to use their voice. It is important to be sensitive to the opponent's right to a fair chance to return the shot. It is good sportsmanship to keep silent when your opponent is playing the point. It is also important to know when to call a hindrance to stand up for your own right to a fair chance.

CHAPTER 8

What Is It Like to Be in the "Zone" or Experience That "Flow"?

When this "tuned-in" state called the Zone is experienced, you begin to feel how your body and mind are working together like a finely tuned machine. It feels effortless. Time is nonexistent. For the duration that you are able to maintain this, you feel like you are functioning in another dimension, almost dreamlike. All the factors in the dimension where we normally exist seem to be frozen in place. We move independently. We are able to influence that "frozen" dimension at will, as if we are not at all affected by the rules of that universe.

That sounds a little mystical and may be a little bit idealistic for the average competitive athlete. When professionals are asked if they experience this altered state and what it is like for them their responses are amazingly similar to the description above. They often add, "I was playing out of my mind." I think they mean to say that it was like their mind was not consciously directing things. They were just feeling the Flow. Maybe the professionals are somehow better able to use the principles outlined here to get to that state. Maybe that is how they got to be as good as they are as professionals. Athletic prowess might be more than just strength and agility. Perhaps those who rise to the top take their physical prowess and combine it with mental skills for an unbeatable combination.

If you begin to focus on these principles, there is no guarantee that you will be "top dog" in tennis or pickleball. I do think you will agree that the people we see winning have an uncanny way of being able to operate on a different plain from the rest of the world. I hope that this book will take you to that optimum plain of performance more often and that you too can discover what it is like to play a winning game consistently.

As a final question after all of this discussion, what is a mind game? Is it something that we inflict on our opponents to gain a tactical advantage? That's probably what most people think of first when they hear the term. I hope that, after this review, the term has taken on new meaning for you. I hope that you now view the term as an aspect of athletic ability similar to your ground game or your net game. With that new perspective, perhaps you will begin to hone your skills in that area and realize a quantum leap forward in your performance and in your overall enjoyment of your chosen sport.

APPENDIX I

Practice Drills

The objective of these drills is to develop the ability to intentionally shift brain states from left to right. Since most of us are left-brain dominant by nature, it is likely that it will be more natural to shift from right to left. Shifting to the right is more of a challenge and requires practice. *Playing right-brain dominant* is the key to playing in the Zone.

Functional Chart

Left-Brain Hemisphere	I	Right-Brain Hemisphere
Sequential processing	I	Visuospatial processing
Verbal/graphical	I	Almost mute
Logical	I	Emotional/feelings
=====Leave here ======>		***********Go Here*********

Earlier we used the example of learning to ride a unicycle to illustrate the function of each brain state as we learn. This time let's go back to childhood to clarify our point. Learning to play in a right-brain-activated state can also be compared to learning to ride a bicycle as a child. If you can remember that far back, when you first became interested in bike riding you probably watched the older kids riding freely. It appeared to be very easy. They were having fun in what looked like an effortless activity.

When you made your first attempt at riding your bike, you kept your left brain in control. You told yourself things like "keep pedaling" and "turn the handlebars" to maintain balance. Your mom or dad probably started you off with those thoughts to keep you upright. After many wobbly trials and plenty of encouragement from your parents there came that magic moment. The turning, leaning and pedaling all came together. It just felt right to take a chance and let yourself feel the balance and the movements. After allowing that shift to the right and then reinforcing the memory of the motions with several hours of practice, you became one of those kids having fun in effortless fashion.

After that transformation happens, rarely do we go back to that thinking stage again. We just know how to ride. That is to say, we know what it feels like to ride and our body responds out of previously recorded experiences of what that sensation feels like. Intuitively we know that allowing our feelings to dominate is a much better way to go.

Sports that involve complex movements like tennis and pickleball draw us back to the left side. There always seems to be an aspect of our mechanics that can be improved. We are required to think about things like shot selection and match strategy, all of which are focused in the left hemisphere.

Knowing that the sport is multifaceted in that way, the player who finds a way to shift gears intentionally from left to right will maximize their performance. Once you do this intentionally and actually *experience* the performance boost, *you will begin to assimilate the feelings associated with playing that way.* It will become natural just like the experience of the carefree kid on the bike. Unfortunately, it won't happen if you allow yourself to stay in the left side. Take care of those facets of the game that are left brained (logical, sequential and verbal) and once they have been addressed learn how to let go. Intentionally go to your feeling right side. Recall the feeling of the shot to be executed when you did it perfectly in the past. As the experience plays back, allow your body to flow with those feelings.

Just as the kids on their bicycles don't go back to the verbal reminders of what to do to stay upright, you will begin to get comfortable playing out of your feeling right side. It will become very natural and it will become a priority to actively make that mental shift. Many in the field of clinical psychology believe that "authentic transformation," or real internal psychological change, occurs as we take the step of faith to apply a truth to our own lives. It is when we experience the fact that the new/true way of thinking or behaving actually does work for us that we allow it to become a part of who we are. Authentic transformation (real internal change) occurs as we experience the fact that it is indeed true not only intellectually, but also for us personally as well. We then assimilate that true way of behaving as our own.

Use these drills to bring about authentic transformation in your game.

Drill #1 The Serve

Start training your brain to switch between the right and left hemispheres with the serve. This is the one time in the game that you can control when the motion happens. You're initiating not reacting.

The goal is to experience the difference between performing with left-brain dominance versus right-brain dominance and to establish the preferred brain state.

First, practice your service motion with many repetitions before you even arrive at the practice court. This is the time to work on mechanics. Study the motion by watching a high-level player. Repeat the motion that you are striving for over and over until it is automatic.

1. When you are ready to begin on the court, do a quick review of your mechanics by going through the motions a few times. Now make a deliberate decision to begin a mental shift.

2. Tell yourself that you have done your rehearsal of mechanics as part of your preparation and leave it in the past. (You can do this because you know what it feels like.)

3. Find your target. At first, aim for the center of the court. Later, as you develop your mental skills, choose smaller targets to build shot control.

4. Visualize the shot going to the target.

5. If you want to try to incorporate a physical stimulus to the cross wiring in your nervous system do so now. Manipulation of the ball in your nondominant hand feeling the texture of the surface of the ball is a good technique.

6. Play in your mind the feelings associated with the optimum motion as they are recorded in your memory of past successful serves. Don't proceed until you feel it.
7. Execute the shot just the way you feel it.

After each attempt, verbally report the statistics to your partner. For example, "That's three for four." Make a value judgment like, "75 percent of my serves have gone in and that's pretty good."

Repeat the above process ten times then switch with your partner.

As you become more skilled at switching mind states intentionally, you might notice that some serves still go astray. In my experience, there will be dramatically fewer errors. When an error occurs, take the time to review in your mind what happened. It's likely that you hurried through your shot, skipping step numbers 5 and 6. I believe this happens to us at first simply because we are not in the habit of performing these steps. Most of us are accustomed to playing out of left-brain dominance. This is why repetition is very important. As you force yourself to execute all these steps and find out through experience that your reliability has dramatically improved, this routine will be assimilated into your game. The quantum leap is realized.

Drill #2 The Rally

A rally, by definition, is when the ball is hit back and forth across the net. A rally is a challenge to the player who wants to play with right-brain dominance because the action is ongoing. Play is reaction and is based on how the ball is hit from the other side of the court. There is no time for rituals and routines.

The idea in this action-oriented situation is to monitor your behavior on an ongoing basis and make changes as necessary. Start a feedback loop to sense trouble and adjust your mental behavior in real time (as it is actually happening). You can prepare prior to the rally by relaxing using controlled breathing. Use a physical stimulus like a slap on your left thigh. As play occurs, begin the feedback loop.

1. What do you sense is playing in your mind? Are you hearing words like "Oh cr—. There I go again!" or any of the other brain-state violations that were identified earlier?

2. If so, do something that is called thought stopping in clinical settings. Once the thought is identified, intentionally stop it from playing.

3. Quickly replace it with what you want to play. In this case, we want to move to a state of right-brain dominance. In place of the left-brain message that was controlling things, intentionally play something very simple to give your left brain something to do that will not dominate. Choose something very easy and to the point. Try just saying the word "feeling." While that word is playing, access your memories of the "feeling" associated with the rhythm of the game when everything is clicking effortlessly.

4. Ask yourself if you are feeling that effortless Zone of performance? If so, enjoy it and stay in that Zone. If not go back to step 1.

To strengthen this routine in your mind and establish it as a good way to play, prepare as outlined above and then hit back and forth with your playing partner with the objective of keeping the ball in play as long as you can. Listen to the activity in your mind. Identify and replace any messages that are violations as they occur. Don't be discouraged if these messages come one after the other. Tell yourself the truth about the messages. The reason that they are coming up so often is that, prior to this exercise, they had free reign in your mind. This procedure will allow you to exert a new level of control and clear away what was once clutter getting in the way of peak performance.

Remember, it's not enough just to have insight regarding how the right and left hemispheres of our brain influence our potential for success in athletics. Repetition in practice is what makes it a reality in your game.

As you get comfortable with the process of stopping the interfering messages and playing the feelings associated with your best play, the habit will become a part of you. The quantum leap will be realized in the rest of your game.

Drill #3 The EX-RAY for Off-court Brain Training (excerpt from MindAlive.com)

The EX-RAY technique allows you to "see" through the blocks of destructive thoughts, conditioned responses, and associations—to see straight into success through your creative imagination. The EX-RAY is a simple five-minute technique similar to other visualization techniques used by Olympic athletes. The athlete identifies the exceptional feelings he/she has had during previous events or practice sessions when he/she performed above his/her normal level of performance. Practicing this exercise can help a peak performer stay at the top of the bell curve more consistently during events when stress is higher. The EX-RAY can also be used for increasing performance when learning, public speaking, during recitals and perfecting any skill.

E—Think of an **E**vent when your performance was exceptional.
X—Feel the e**X**ceptional feelings and thoughts you had during this event.
R—**R**ecall these exceptional qualities with all of your senses and feelings.
A—**A**llow these exceptional qualities from the exceptional event to fill your body and mind as you apply them to the new event you are about to become part of.
Y—Say **Y**es! As you see through your obstacles and feel your success in the upcoming event that you have just witnessed in your mind.

Repeat this process as often as needed. For increased effectiveness, use EX-RAY along with the skill-development session (AVE).
When the session speeds up (after about ten minutes), visualize
doing the actions of the actual event until the session ends.

REAL LIFE EXAMPLES

This section is intended to provide some real-life experiences with this method as they are reported back to us from our readers. We can all learn from each other as we develop our new mind game. As we see the methods implemented we will report back to our community of players here and in the testimonials section of our web site. (See www.mindgame. guru) (report your experiences to admin@mindgame.guru).

8/27/16 Player from Preston, CT

Our first example occurred as the author was on vacation in the Northeast. It was a great vacation. I had an opportunity to play pickleball in three states (Connecticut, Rhode Island and Massachusetts). I used the web site (USAPA.org) to find places to play in the area. This is a useful function available to anyone traveling in the United States. I also contacted a fellow ambassador who is from Rhode Island, Jim Labrosse. He was a gracious host. As usual in Pickleball clubs across the nation, I was accepted immediately and made to feel like I was a part of their family. I continue to be impressed by the sense of camaraderie among pickleball players.

For the most part, regarding their skill level, these players were high 3.5 to 4.0 and above. It was obvious that most of them had been playing pickleball for several years. Most had experience with other racket sports before that. On one of the days of hard fought doubles matches a problem came up. One of the players started missing her serve. She had been hitting shots that most players only dream about. Unfortunately, when came her turn to serve it was like she had never played before. She became more and more frustrated as the number of missed serves accumulated.

As I watched her grow more and more frustrated I asked myself, "If not now, when"? "If not me then who"? Actually, it wasn't that dramatic. I asked her for permission to share with her some tricks that I have learned that can help. I reviewed some of the basic principles of playing with a mind game. She seemed hesitant but was cautiously receptive and gave it a try.

We didn't have a lot of time so we kept it fairly simple. The idea of right and left brain functionality was introduced. Using the cross wiring of the nervous system to stimulate the right brain was covered. The sequence of finding her target, aiming at her target, **feeling the shot** and then letting it go was reviewed and repeated several times.

She gave it a try right away. Her next three serves went in and hit the area that she was targeting. The grim and frustrated facial expression gave way to a bright smile.

NOTE TO THE READER

Please stay in touch with us via our website http://www.mindgame.guru. Send us your story about how you have used these ideas and whether you would like to share your experiences with other players. It's a great way to connect with others who are using these methods. All of us will benefit from sharing tricks that we have found to be useful.

Look up Mind Game on Facebook. Don't forget to "like" us. We want to build a community of players who use this technique with the objective of sharing results.

FURTHER READING

Bourne, E. 1997. *The Anxiety & Phobia Workbook*. Oakland, CA: New Harbinger Publications.

Childre, D. 1991–2016. *Heart Math*. Boulder Creek, CA. http://www.heart-math.com.

Childre, D. 1998. *Freeze Frame*. Boulder Creek, CA: Planetary Publications.

Corvallis, P. 2003. *Visuospatial Processing and the Right Hemisphere Interpreter*. Hanover, NH: Center for Cognitive Neuroscience, Dartmouth College. http://www.sciencedirect.com.

Forman, J., and D. Myers. 1987. *The Personal Stress Reduction Program*. Englewood Cliffs, NJ: Prentice Hall.

Matheny, K., and R. Riordan.1992. *Stress and Strategies for Lifestyle Management*. Atlanta, GA: Georgia State University Business Press.

Siever, D. 2016. Edmonton, AB. http://www.mindalive.com.

Shapiro, F. 2001. *Eye Movement Desensitization and Reprocessing EMDR*. New York: Guilford Press.

NOTES - HOW AND WHY

The following pages have been provided to facilitate the readers experience in observing and correcting mental states effectively. Making note taking a part of training provides a level of assurance that practice and match experiences will contribute to the overall process of raising your level of play.

Without this discipline, most opportunities for learning go by without benefit. There may be an observation that things were going extraordinarily well or poorly, but without an understanding of what may have contributed to the situation. Make this a part of your training and you will be rewarded with more productive practice sessions.

First of all, since note taking is a left brained function, perform this task at the right time. Make sure that you don't interrupt play or your drills since this will draw you out of the Zone. Instead, soon after the action is over, review in your mind what you experienced. For example, when things went wrong, make a note regarding your mental state? Did you go through all the steps of preparing mentally including accessing the feelings associated with that shot? When the spectacular put-away shot was executed during the rally, were you using the feed-back loop to manage your mental state? If so, what thoughts were intercepted? What did that great shot feel like?

Another example might be the experience of trying to end a rally with a winner unsuccessfully. You might review the experience in your mind and remember that you had noticed muscle tension. Going further with the memory, you may recall that there was some banter initiated by one of your opponents. Instead of calling for a hindrance and resetting mentally, you tried to intensify your focus and play through the situation. The result was a fault and a lost opportunity to maintain your momentum. Tensing up and trying increase your focus was not a winning strategy. The next time this comes up you may be more likely to guard you place in the Zone and keep your momentum going.

The objective is to develop and strengthen your skills in moving in and out of the Zone by observing when it happens and when is does not. It will also encourage you to set a high priority on your mental game, eventually bringing it to the forefront of who you are on court. This is what it takes to become that player who is known as a "back-board". Every shot that is hit to that person seems to come back to the opponent. This is the work required to develop the reputation that when things get tough you just get tougher.

Use these pages to facilitate a quantum leap improvement in performance and become all that you can be. Remember, knowledge of how to manage your brain state without practice and thoughtful evaluation is much like reading about how to hit an overhead (or any other shot for that matter) and then never swinging your racket or paddle.

Stay loose. Swing freely. Experience your shots via your right brain and enjoy the thrill of advancing to ever higher levels of play.

Notes

Notes

Notes

Notes

About the Author

Neil P. Schulenburg, PhD, is a psychotherapist specializing in memory resolution in trauma recovery. He uses the adaptive information processing theory and cognitive behavioral theory. Dr. Schulenburg is published in the Journal of Neurotherapy and has several eBooks available. He is a board-certified professional counselor and certified EMDR therapist.

Dr. Schulenburg has received degrees from Georgia State University, the Psychological Studies Institute, and Logos Christian College and Graduate School.

Dr. Schulenburg has always had a passion for tennis. He is a member of the United States Tennis Association (USTA) and the Atlanta Lawn Tennis Association (ALTA). In 2015, he became a United States of America Pickleball Association (USAPA) Ambassador. He won the gold and silver medals in the Georgia State Senior Olympics in singles and doubles pickleball.

Made in the USA
Las Vegas, NV
21 May 2021